My State
RHODE ISLAND

By Christina Earley

TABLE OF CONTENTS

A Crabtree Seedlings Book

Crabtree Publishing
crabtreebooks.com

School-to-Home Support for Caregivers and Teachers

This book helps children grow by letting them practice reading. Here are a few guiding questions to help the reader build his or her comprehension skills. Possible answers appear in red.

Before Reading:

- What do I know about Rhode Island?
  - *I know that Rhode Island is a state.*
  - *I know that Rhode Island has beaches.*

- What do I want to learn about Rhode Island?
  - *I want to learn which famous people were born in Rhode Island.*
  - *I want to learn what the state flag looks like.*

During Reading:

- What have I learned so far?
  - *I have learned that Providence is the state capital of Rhode Island.*
  - *I have learned that there are more than 30 islands in Narragansett Bay.*

- I wonder why...
  - *I wonder why the state flower is the common blue violet.*
  - *I wonder why there is an anchor on Rhode Island's state flag.*

After Reading:

- What did I learn about Rhode Island?
  - *I have learned that there is a merry-go-round at Watch Hill.*
  - *I have learned that the state animal is the harbor seal.*

- Read the book again and look for the glossary words.
  - *I see the word **capital** on page 6, and the word **anchor** on page 12. The other glossary words are found on pages 22 and 23.*

RHODE ISLAND
Hi! My name is Theo. Welcome to Rhode Island!

I live in Newport. It is on an **island**.

Newport had the first **ferry** service in the U.S.!

Rhode Island is in the northeastern United States. The **capital** is Providence.

Fun Fact: Providence is the largest city in Rhode Island.

The state animal is the harbor seal.

The common blue violet is the state flower.

We grow a lot of corn in Rhode Island. Some of it is used to make corn on the cob.

Fun Fact: Rhode Island grows 42,000 tons (38,100 metric tons) of corn a year.

My state flag is white. It has a gold **anchor** in the middle, surrounded by 13 stars.

I like to visit the Breakers. It is a beautiful house built in the late 1800s that is now a **museum**.

I enjoy surfing with my family at Narragansett **Bay**.

Fun Fact: There are more than 30 islands in Narragansett Bay.

Riding the horses on the Watch Hill merry-go-round is one of my favorite things to do!

I like to learn about the history of tennis at the International Tennis Hall of Fame.

Actor Robert Capron, who starred in the movie *Diary of a Wimpy Kid,* was born in Rhode Island. Olympic swimmer Elizabeth Beisel was also born in Rhode Island.

Fun Fact: Businesswoman Carolyn Rafaelian was born in Providence, Rhode Island.

The view of the Atlantic Ocean is beautiful along the Cliff Walk.

It is fun to hike through the forest in Arcadia.

Glossary

anchor (ayn-ker): A heavy hooked object attached to a boat or ship that is dropped into the water to hold it in place

bay (bay): A large area of water that is connected to an ocean or lake and that is partly surrounded by land

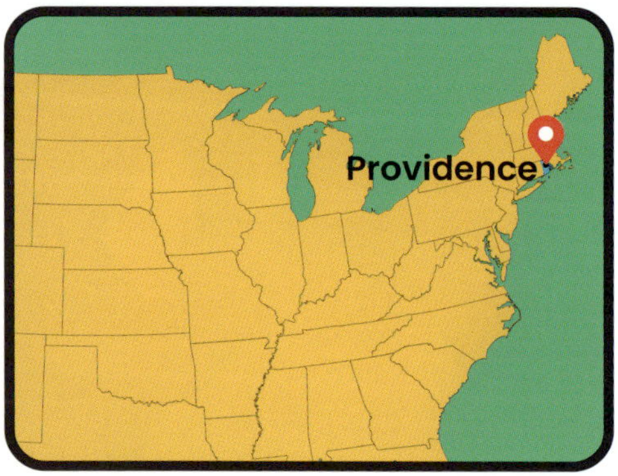

capital (cap-ih-tuhl): The city or town where the government of a country, state, or province is located

ferry (fay-ree): A boat that is used to carry passengers over a short distance

island (ie-luhnd): Land that is completely surrounded by water

museum (mew-zee-uhm): A place where interesting and valuable things are collected for people to see

Index

About the Author

Christina Earley lives in sunny South Florida with her husband and son. She enjoys traveling around the United States and learning about different historical places. Her hobbies include hiking, yoga, and baking.

Written by: Christina Earley
Designed and Illustrated by: Bobbie Houser
Series Development: James Earley
Proofreader: Melissa Boyce
Educational Consultant: Marie Lemke M.Ed.

Photographs:
Alamy: Stephen Vincent: p. 5, 23; Tom Croke: p. 16; WENN Rights Ltd: p. 18 left; Abaca Press: p. 18 right; WENN Rights Ltd: p. 19; George Ostertag: p. 21
Shutterstock: Jim Schubert: cover; Jane Damiani: p. 3; Felix Lipov: p. 4, 23; Volina: p. 6, 22; Sean Pavone: p. 7; Martin Prochazkacz: p. 8; Predrag Lukic: p. 9; chanwangrong: p. 10-11; Ken Felepchuk: p. 11; railway fx: p. 12, 22; Dan Hanscom: p. 13, 23; The Global Guy: p. 14-15, 22; solepsizm: p. 15; Joy Brown: p. 17; KYPhua: p. 20

Crabtree Publishing

crabtreebooks.com 800-387-7650

Printed in the U.S.A./072023/CG20230214

Published in Canada
Crabtree Publishing
616 Welland Avenue
St. Catharines, Ontario
L2M 5V6

Published in the United States
Crabtree Publishing
347 Fifth Avenue
Suite 1402-145
New York, New York, 10016

Library and Archives Canada Cataloguing in Publication
Available at Library and Archives Canada

Library of Congress Cataloging-in-Publication Data
Available at the Library of Congress

Hardcover: 978-1-0398-0533-0
Paperback: 978-1-0398-0565-1
Ebook (pdf): 978-1-0398-0629-0
Epub: 978-1-0398-0597-2